ARMIES OF THE PAST

GOING TO WAR IN
WORLD
WAR TWO

ARMIES OF THE PAST

GOING TO WAR IN
WORLD
WAR TWO

MOIRA BUTTERFIELD

W

FRANKLIN WATTS

LONDON • SYDNEY

ILLUSTRATIONS BY

Mark Bergin
Kevin Maddison
Lee Montgomery
Peter Visscher
Mike White
Maps by Stefan Chabluk

Editor Penny Clarke
Editor-in-Chief John C. Miles

Designer Steve Prosser
Art Director Jonathan Hair
Picture Research Susan Mennell

© 2001 Franklin Watts

First published in 2001
by Franklin Watts
96 Leonard Street
London
EC2A 4XD

Franklin Watts Australia
56 O'Riordan Street
Alexandria
NSW 2015

ISBN 0 7496 4043 X

Dewey classification: 940.53

A CIP catalogue record
for this book is available
from the British Library.

Printed in Hong Kong, China

CONTENTS

The road to war

In 1918 Germany lost World War One and was forced to sign the Treaty of Versailles. The treaty took land from Germany, made the country pay reparations (money compensation) for the war and banned it from having armed forces. These rules were very unpopular with Germans, so in 1933 they supported a new leader, Adolf Hitler, who promised to break the treaty. He led a political party called the National Socialists, or Nazis.

The Nazis began to rearm Germany and demand the return of territory. Britain and France tried to negotiate with Hitler, but he ignored them and began to seize land. This triggered World War Two, a conflict that involved many countries and lasted from 1939 to 1945.

CANADA

USA

Battle of the Atlantic 1939-45

ATLANT OCEAN

Fascist beliefs
The Nazis were fascists, which means they ruled by military power. They believed in extreme nationalism – that their country should rule over others.

Hitler was a dictator. Although initially elected, by 1939 he had ruthlessly imposed his will and eliminated anyone who opposed him. The symbol of his Nazi party was the swastika.

CHRONOLOGY OF THE WAR

1939
September: Germany invades Poland. War is declared by Britain, France, Australia, New Zealand and Canada.

German leader Adolf Hitler

1940
German troops advance through Europe and conquer most of France. Italy enters the war. Battle of Britain. The Blitz begins.

British Prime Minister Winston Churchill

1941
Germans advance in North Africa and the USSR. Japan attacks Pearl Harbor and the USA enters the war.

US President Franklin Roosevelt

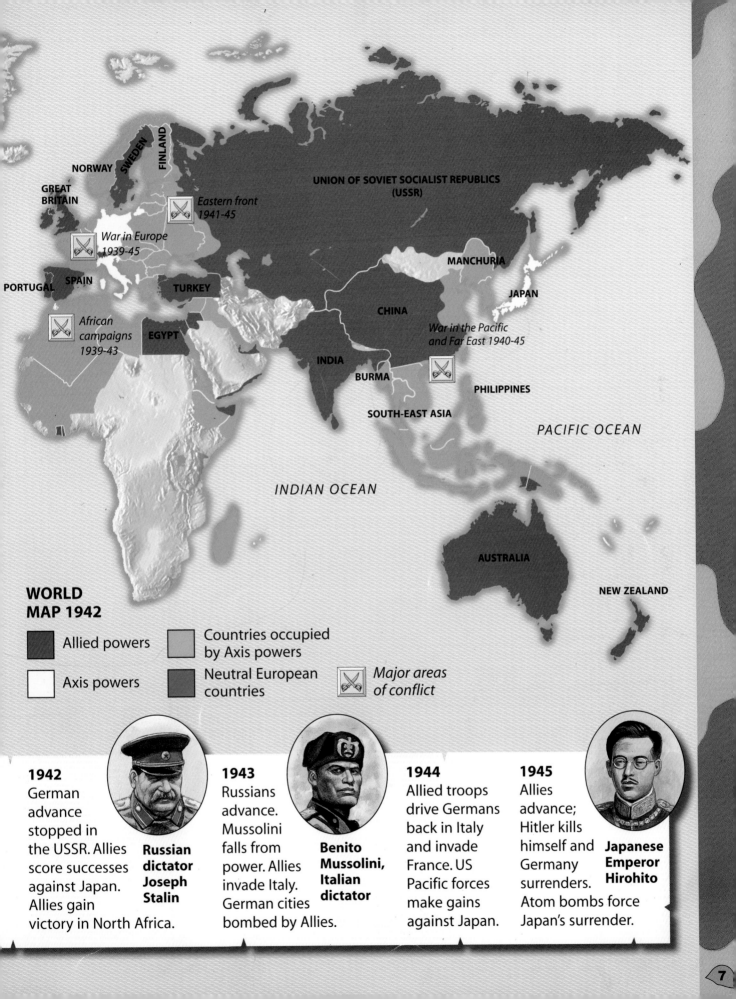

NORWAY

SWEDEN

FINLAND

GREAT
BRITAIN

UNION OF SOVIET SOCIALIST REPUBLICS
(USSR)

Eastern front
1941–45

War in Europe
1939–45

MANCHURIA

PORTUGAL

SPAIN

TURKEY

JAPAN

African
campaigns
1939–43

EGYPT

CHINA

War in the Pacific
and Far East 1940–45

INDIA

BURMA

PHILIPPINES

SOUTH-EAST ASIA

PACIFIC OCEAN

INDIAN OCEAN

AUSTRALIA

NEW ZEALAND

WORLD MAP 1942

- Allied powers
- Axis powers
- Countries occupied by Axis powers
- Neutral European countries
- *Major areas of conflict*

1942
German advance stopped in the USSR. Allies score successes against Japan. Allies gain victory in North Africa.

Russian dictator Joseph Stalin

1943
Russians advance. Mussolini falls from power. Allies invade Italy. German cities bombed by Allies.

Benito Mussolini, Italian dictator

1944
Allied troops drive Germans back in Italy and invade France. US Pacific forces make gains against Japan.

1945
Allies advance; Hitler kills himself and Germany surrenders. Atom bombs force Japan's surrender.

Japanese Emperor Hirohito

Blitzkrieg!

On 1 September 1939, 1.25 million German troops – many in tanks and military vehicles – swept into Poland as the German air force knocked out the Polish air force in the skies above. The German advance was fast and effective. It was a new kind of fighting – one that replaced the trench-based warfare of World War One, when armies dug in and battled for weeks in the same place.

During 1939 and 1940 German forces spread across Europe, over-running France, the Netherlands, Norway, Denmark, Luxembourg and Belgium.

They seemed unstoppable.

NETHERLANDS, BELGIUM AND FRANCE 1939-40

← Main route of German attack
← Other German attacks

ALLIES AND AXIS POWERS

The Nazis were allied with Italy and Japan. Together they were called the Axis powers. The countries that fought against them were known as the Allies.

During 1939-40 the USSR stayed friendly with Hitler. The USA did not go to war, but instead supplied the Allies with equipment such as ships.

German tanks, such as this one, spearheaded Blitzkrieg invasion forces.

FAST FIGHTING
The new German fighting tactic was called *Blitzkrieg*, meaning 'lightning war'. As dive-bomber aircraft attacked targets such as railway lines, ground forces and artillery (heavy guns) moved rapidly forward to cut off and encircle enemy armies, forcing them to surrender. This type of warfare relied heavily on tanks and other motorised vehicles.

'Thus we begin our march into the great German future.'

Hitler on the invasion of Czechoslovakia, 1938

DISASTER AT DUNKIRK

Britain sent a large army, the British Expeditionary Force, to assist France. But in June 1940 the troops had to retreat to the coast at Dunkirk in northern France. As German aeroplanes attacked, an armada of vessels evacuated 340,000 troops.

Destroyers, ferries and even little fishing boats and pleasure craft took part. Anyone with a boat who could find their way across the English Channel went to the rescue.

Long lines of British and French troops wait to be evacuated from the beaches at Dunkirk.

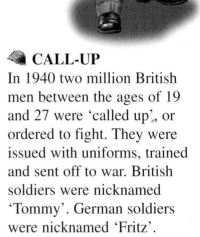

A British recruit dresses in his newly issued uniform.

CALL-UP

In 1940 two million British men between the ages of 19 and 27 were 'called up', or ordered to fight. They were issued with uniforms, trained and sent off to war. British soldiers were nicknamed 'Tommy'. German soldiers were nicknamed 'Fritz'.

BLITZKRIEG FORCES

WEHRMACHT

German army ground forces were called the *Wehrmacht*. Hitler was in overall command of them.

LUFTWAFFE

The German air force was called the *Luftwaffe*. In the 1930s, Germany had built it into a formidable weapon.

THE SS

There was a separate army of ruthless military police called the SS. They enforced Nazi rule in the occupied countries.

Battle in the sky

After France fell in June 1940, Britain and her allies stood alone against Hitler. He planned to invade Britain, but first he sent the *Luftwaffe* to destroy Britain's Royal Air Force (RAF). Without the RAF, Britain would have been an easier conquest.

During the summer of 1940, the Battle of Britain raged in the skies over Britain and RAF fighters fought to the death with the *Luftwaffe*. The RAF narrowly won the contest and Hitler postponed his invasion. Instead he sent aircraft to rain down bombs on Britain's cities, a tactic known as the 'Blitz'.

London blazes during the Blitz.

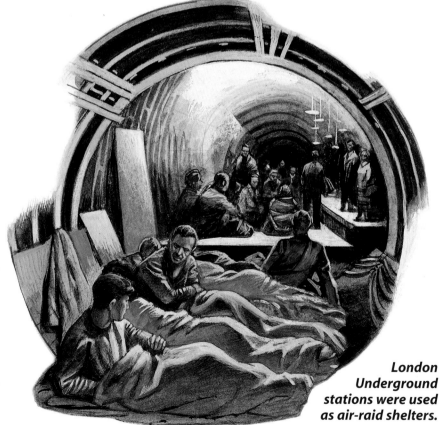

London Underground stations were used as air-raid shelters.

WINTER TERROR
Between September 1940 and May 1941 the *Luftwaffe* made nightly bombing raids on many British cities. Thousands were killed or injured.

FIRE!
Enemy aircraft dropped tonnes of high-explosive and incendiary bombs. Incendiaries started fires that spread quickly, causing terrible damage.

AIR RAID ALERT!
Wailing sirens signalled that enemy bombers were on the way. People rushed to underground air-raid shelters and stayed there until they heard an 'all-clear' siren.

RADAR

Radar (RAdio Detection And Ranging) was invented just before the war. Britain had a good system that could detect approaching enemy aircraft. It was a big advantage in the Battle of Britain.

'Never in the field of human conflict was so much owed by so many to so few.'

Winston Churchill praises the RAF, 1940

RAF LIFE

Throughout 1940, young Allied pilots were quickly trained to take the place of those killed. At their British bases, they awaited the call to 'scramble' – rush to their aeroplanes and take off to meet the incoming enemy.

Crews on the ground kept the planes flying; the Women's Auxiliary Air Force remained in radio contact with the pilots and passed on messages.

An RAF fighter pilot in flying kit, including helmet and parachute

British Hurricane and Spitfire fighter aircraft attack a German Junkers Ju-88 during the Battle of Britain.

THE BATTLE OF BRITAIN

The Battle of Britain is the name given to the *Luftwaffe's* attempt to destroy RAF Fighter Command, which lasted from July to September 1940. Aerial battles took place between single-seater fighter aeroplanes; both air forces suffered heavy losses of men and machines. But the RAF just managed to survive and eventually the *Luftwaffe* had to reduce its raids.

New battlegrounds

In June 1941 Hitler attacked the USSR. Until that time the two countries had agreed not to fight, and the USSR's Red Army was taken by surprise when tanks and thousands of troops crossed the border.

Meanwhile, the USA still held back from going to war, although President Roosevelt was trying hard to persuade his country to help. All that changed when Japanese forces attacked the US naval base at Pearl Harbor, Hawaii. By the end of 1941, the Allies were joined by two large and powerful friends – the USSR and the USA.

Japanese soldier

WAR IN THE SNOW

The area of fighting between Germany and the USSR was called the 'Eastern Front'. In winter it was bitterly cold and the German troops found the terrible conditions hard to cope with. Russian troops were better prepared, with warm white suits that camouflaged (hid) them.

Battle raged during 1941 and 1942 with huge losses of troops and equipment on both sides. It was a big drain on Hitler's resources.

A Red Army soldier equipped for winter in a snow suit

PACIFIC TENSION

Japan began to expand in the Pacific region throughout the 1930s. By annexing (invading) territory, they intended eventually to conquer India and Australia and create a giant new empire in alliance with the Nazis.

'Each regiment lost about 400 men to frostbite. The tanks could barely move … Our weapons jammed in the cold.'

A German general recalls the winter of 1941 in the USSR.

FIGHTING FRIENDS

Troops from many countries fought on the Allied side. Among them were soldiers from Australia and New Zealand (ANZACs), Canada, India and South Africa. Many people who had escaped from defeated countries also fought with the Allies.

Within Nazi-occupied countries, people tried to sabotage their new rulers and help trapped Allied soldiers to escape. These brave, secret helpers were called resistance fighters. If caught, some were tortured to make them reveal the names of their colleagues. Others were sent to prison camps or shot by Nazi firing squads.

Canadian (left) and Australian soldiers

ATTACK ON THE USA

On 7 December 1941 wave after wave of Japanese warplanes attacked the giant US naval fleet moored at Pearl Harbor, Hawaii. The USA was taken by surprise. Ships and planes were destroyed; more than 2,400 people were killed.

Americans were outraged and finally agreed with their President that the USA should enter the war. The United States had so many troops and so much equipment that eventually its entry into the war helped tip the balance against the Axis countries.

Japanese forces attack Pearl Harbor on 7 December 1941. This early colour photograph shows American warships ablaze.

Wolfpacks and warships

During the war merchant ships crossed the North Atlantic from the USA and Canada, bringing vital supplies of food and equipment to Europe. The German navy used U-boats (submarines) to destroy as many of the ships as possible before they arrived. This fiercely fought contest on the high seas was named the Battle of the Atlantic.

SEA WOLVES

Merchant ships travelled in large groups called convoys, escorted for protection by Allied warships.

The Germans hunted them with armed U-boats. These often travelled in groups nicknamed 'wolfpacks'.

HMS Belfast, a Royal Navy World War Two battlecruiser now moored on the River Thames in London

Radar

Two 6-inch triple gun turrets

Bridge

Anti-aircraft guns protected the ship from aerial attack

ALLIED FORCES

Convoys were escorted by aircraft and by destroyers and other warships. They hunted U-boats by dropping depth charges, bombs that exploded at a pre-set depth underwater. They also had a good sonar (sound-based) submarine detection system called ASDIC. In the end, these advantages gave the Allies the upper hand over the U-boats.

'The enemy, by means of new location devices... makes fighting impossible.'

Admiral Dönitz, commander of the German navy, complains about Allied radar and sonar.

WAR AT SEA

MINE DANGER

Both sides laid explosive sea mines. Some floated underwater on wires. Others sat on the sea bed, triggered by sound. Minesweeping ships had the job of clearing them away.

BROKEN CODE

The British navy captured a U-boat and found material on board that helped them to break a code, called 'Enigma', that the Germans used to send secret messages. This helped the Allies work out where U-boats were positioned.

BAD NEWS AT SEA

It was a great blow to morale when a famous warship was sunk. On the Allied side the loss of HMS *Hood* in 1941 made terrible news. More than 1,400 men died. On the German side the loss of the *Graf Spee* in 1939 (above), and the *Bismarck* in 1941 stood out as awful disasters.

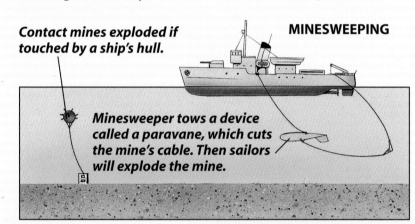

Contact mines exploded if touched by a ship's hull.

MINESWEEPING

Minesweeper tows a device called a paravane, which cuts the mine's cable. Then sailors will explode the mine.

GERMAN FORCES

The *Kriegsmarine* (German navy) attacked with U-boats and pocket battleships (cruisers with heavy guns). It also had some very large ships, such as the *Bismarck*, which was sunk in 1941.

LIFE ON BOARD

Life for a sailor was tough, and thousands of naval and merchant crewmen were killed. Sailors lived in small spaces below deck, often sharing a hammock with someone on a different watch (work-shift). Allied sailors lived with the fear of a surprise U-boat attack. U-boat crews were terrified of an attack from surface ships.

An Allied convoy

War in the Pacific

Both the Japanese and US navies fought fiercely in the Pacific. They used naval task forces – groups of aircraft carriers escorted by destroyers, submarines and battleships. Other ships were loaded with troops for onshore fighting.

At first Japan occupied many Pacific islands but US forces later drove them back island by island in a series of bitter and bloody battles. Japan was led throughout the war by its generals, with the emperor, Hirohito, at their head.

Japanese Kamikaze aircraft

KAMIKAZE!
In 1944 the Japanese started using suicide pilots called *Kamikaze*. They deliberately crashed their explosive-packed planes onto enemy ships.

AMPHIBIOUS ATTACKS
The US navy sent their naval soldiers, the Marines, ashore on special landing vehicles that could carry troops or cargo such as tanks. They spearheaded the fight in the Pacific, landing on the islands occupied by the Japanese. It was a tough task; the Japanese were fanatical fighters who hated to surrender.

US Marines land from a landing craft on to a beach in the Pacific.

'I shall return.'

General MacArthur's famous promise when US troops had to withdraw from the Philippines early in 1942.

GIANTS OF THE SEA

Aircraft carriers were vital during the Pacific war. Each one was a massive floating airbase as well as a warship bristling with guns. Their strike aircraft could take off and bomb a distant enemy; their fighter aeroplanes could fend off incoming aerial attacks. The US Navy had the most carriers.

HISTORY'S BIGGEST SEA BATTLE

Allied forces were pushed back in the Pacific in early 1942, but they returned and counter-attacked in a series of blistering sea battles. At the Battle of Midway in June, Japan lost four aircraft carriers, and never fully recovered. Unknown to them, the US had cracked their secret radio codes and knew where and when to attack them.

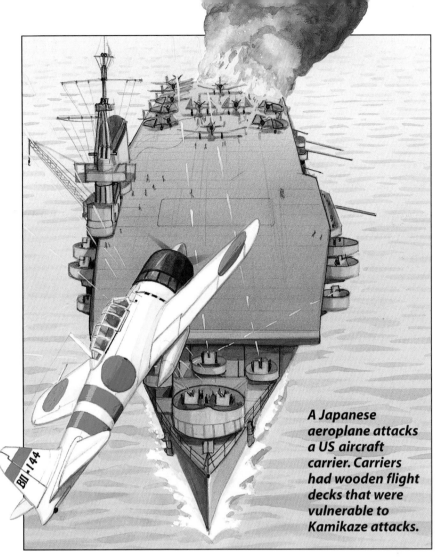

A Japanese aeroplane attacks a US aircraft carrier. Carriers had wooden flight decks that were vulnerable to Kamikaze attacks.

TOUGH TERRAIN

JUNGLE WAR

Britain and Commonwealth troops fought the Japanese in the jungles of Burma and India. There was more hand-to-hand fighting here, as tanks were useless in the dense trees.

AFRICAN DESERTS

Allied troops fought the German and Italian *Afrika Korps* in the deserts of North Africa. Troops there had to deal with extremes of heat and cold. They fought tank battles and tried to knock out fortified enemy positions.

DISEASE DANGER

Jungle fighting conditions were atrocious. Troops had to cope with monsoon rains, blood-sucking leeches and malaria, a disease spread by the bites of the mosquitoes that thrived in the damp conditions.

Life at home

In the war zones many civilian (non-military) people suffered, losing their homes, loved ones and sometimes their lives to enemy bombs.

In Britain life was hard as food and fuel were rationed (their supply was controlled). Although the country was not invaded people called it the 'Home Front', because they felt they were part of the war.

In North America people did not suffer bombs or shortages, but they worked hard to make guns, ships and tanks, and anxiously awaited news of their family and friends fighting far away.

British soldier of the Home Guard

The Sky's the Limit!

KEEP BUYING WAR BONDS

HOME GUARD

Sometimes British men could not join the forces because they were too old, medically unfit or had vital jobs to do at home. Instead, they helped by joining the Home Guard, a part-time group whose volunteers trained to man invasion defences and learn fighting techniques in case the enemy arrived.

YOU CAN HELP!

Government posters encouraged people to buy government bonds to help pay for the war effort, save fuel and keep quiet if they knew anything about troop movements, in case enemy spies were listening.

An American War Bonds poster

WOMEN IN WAR

Women around the world played a vital part in World War Two. They took over many of the jobs once done only by men. They worked in weapons factories, ran emergency services and toiled on farms to boost food production.

In the services they went to the front as nurses; many held important back-up jobs, such as code-breaking. Factories worked around the clock to supply equipment to the forces.

FARM WORKER

FACTORY WORKER

NURSE

AUXILIARY SERVICEWOMAN

'We had to save all kinds of things for the war effort – fat off the roast, rubber bands, tin cans or any kind of scrap metal. It was all collected and went to help make planes and tanks.'

A Canadian woman remembers life in 1942.

PUT OUT THAT LIGHT!

In Britain, the 'blackout' was in effect – no lights were allowed after dark so that *Luftwaffe* bombers could not easily spot their targets. Air-raid wardens patrolled the streets to enforce this rule.

GIs started a new dance craze, the 'jitterbug'.

THE YANKS ARE COMING!

In 1942 US troops began to arrive in Britain, where they trained for fighting on mainland Europe. They brought with them luxuries for local people, such as sweets, chocolate and chewing gum.

Ordinary US troops were called GIs (from the words 'Government Issue' on their equipment). They often held dances at their bases, and these provided a welcome taste of fun and good times in a country that had endured three years of hardship.

Capture and escape

When troops were captured by the enemy they became POWs (prisoners of war). They were sent to high-security prisons called POW camps.

Many POWs tried to escape and get back home. Some succeeded but others were caught. It was a great risk to escape in the USSR or the Far East because recaptured prisoners were often executed. In Germany the SS sometimes executed escaped POWs.

'It is the duty of all captured officers to try to escape.'

British forces official regulation.

Colditz Castle, situated near the River Mulde in Germany

COLDITZ
Colditz Castle in Germany was a famous POW prison. It was meant to be impossible to escape from, but many prisoners did.

BREAKOUT

PLANNING TO ESCAPE
Allied POWs worked hard and in secret to plan their escapes. They managed to make civilian clothes (below), fake passports and money to help them get home.

TUNNELS
Some POWs dug secret tunnels leading outside prison walls (above). The dangerous work could take many months using only makeshift tools. The diggers constantly risked discovery by prison guards.

ON THE RUN
Once they escaped from prison POWs counted on help from local resistance groups to hide them (below) and organise their travel. If these helpers were caught by the Nazis they could be shot.

SECRET SOLDIERS

In occupied Europe (the parts invaded by the Nazis), undercover resistance groups sabotaged factories, trains and ports. Experts were trained in Britain and parachuted in at night.

One of the most dangerous undercover jobs was that of the wireless operator (right) who had to send and receive secret radio messages from London. If operators stayed on the air for too long, the Germans could pick up the signal and find them.

POWs

In the Far East, Allied soldiers and civilians were captured and held prisoner by the Japanese in appalling conditions. They were starved, denied medical aid and forced to do hard slave labour.

Some Allied POWs were forced to work in Japanese mines (left).

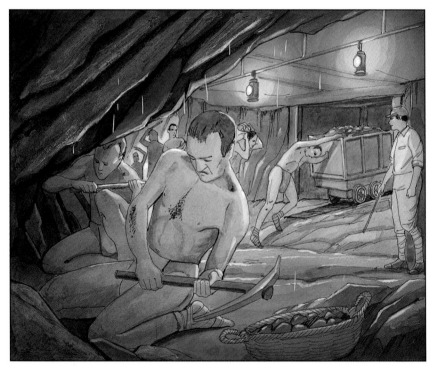

A TERRIBLE SECRET

The Nazis set up brutal prisons, called concentration camps, for those civilians who opposed them or who belonged to minorities such as Jews or gypsies. Millions were killed but the extent of the murders remained secret until Allied troops discovered the camps at the end of the war.

GESTAPO

The secret police section of the SS was called the *Geheime Staatspolizei*, or Gestapo for short. They were greatly feared because they interrogated and tortured captured resistance fighters to make them betray their colleagues.

A Gestapo military policeman

The tide turns

In 1943 the tide of the war turned. Thousands of German and Italian troops were captured in North Africa and the Allies moved towards Italy. On the Eastern Front in the USSR, the biggest land battle in history raged and Hitler's forces were slowly driven back.

Meanwhile German industrial centres were pounded day and night by Allied bombs.

Red Army troops advance at Stalingrad.

Russian T-34 tank

🦊 'DEATH RIDE' OF THE PANZERS

At Kursk the cream of Hitler's Panzers (tank forces) attacked a heavily defended Russian position. It became known as the 'Death Ride' of the Panzers, as the fast T-34 Russian tanks charged into the ranks of German Tiger tanks in the biggest tank battle in history.

On July 12 there was a huge artillery battle between tanks – a ferocity of shelling never seen before or since.

Eventually the Germans withdrew, the strength of their tank forces badly damaged. Many thousands lay dead; the Red Army alone had more than 600,000 casualties.

🦊 AN ARMY SMASHED

German forces moved south to capture the USSR's oilfields, and the German 6th Army entered the city of Stalingrad. But they were trapped and encircled by the Red Army. Cut off from supplies, 300,000 German troops died of cold, starvation or in ferocious hand-to-hand street fighting.

Hitler ordered his troops not to surrender but eventually their commander disobeyed and surrendered to save the last of his men. It was a vital victory for the USSR.

'Za Stalina, Za Rodinu!'
'For Stalin, for the Motherland!'

Red Army battle slogan, scratched on their tank turrets

INVASION OF ITALY

BEACH FIGHTING
Allied troops invaded Sicily and later landed on the Italian mainland. Many of the troops who came ashore encountered fierce gunfire and overhead bombing from German aircraft.

SURRENDER
Italy surrendered on 8 September 1943. Most Italian soldiers gave up or changed sides, but the occupying German forces fought fiercely to hold on to the country.

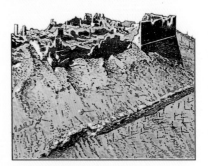

Monte Cassino in ruins

BATTLING ON
The Allies made their way towards Rome but the main route was blocked by the hilltop monastery of Monte Cassino, held by the Germans. It took four months of bitter fighting to dislodge them.

BOMBS NIGHT AND DAY
RAF and US Air Force bombers pulverised German cities and industrial centres with day-and-night bombing raids. The raids were meant to destroy the German war economy and force surrender. Sometimes mass drops of incendiary (fire) bombs created firestorms that swept through city streets, killing thousands.

RAF LANCASTER NIGHT BOMBER

US P-51D MUSTANG FIGHTER

The Mustang had six machine guns mounted in its wings

BOMBER ESCORTS
Squadrons of US bombers on their way to attack Germany were defended by agile P-51 Mustang fighters. The Mustang was the best all-round fighter aircraft of the war, with a top speed of more than 600 km/h.

D-Day

On 6 June 1944 'Operation Overlord' began. Allied troops landed in Normandy, northern France, to begin the liberation of Europe from Nazi forces. It was also called 'D-Day' and was the biggest seaborne assault in history. More than 10,000 planes and 4,000 ships took part, together with 156,000 US, British, Canadian and other Allied soldiers. They landed on five French beaches to open the 'Second Front', the re-invasion of occupied Europe.

PLAN OF BATTLE

Five beaches were chosen for the landings. They were codenamed Omaha, Utah, Juno, Sword and Gold. US troops attacked Omaha and Utah. British and Commonwealth troops took the others. The operation began early in the morning when troops parachuted behind the beaches to secure roads and bridges. Then seaborne troops clambered from their ships into landing craft, while Allied warships bombarded German beach defences with gunfire.

Steel helmet

Rifle

Belt

First aid kit

Entrenching tool

Fighting knife

US INFANTRYMAN

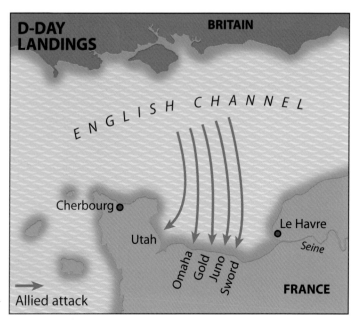

D-DAY LANDINGS

BRITAIN

ENGLISH CHANNEL

Cherbourg

Utah

Omaha
Gold
Juno
Sword

Le Havre

Seine

FRANCE

→
Allied attack

CLEVER ENGINEERING

Some clever new inventions helped the invading Allied armies to land on D-Day.

FLOATING TRUCK

DUKWs (nicknamed 'ducks') were vehicles that worked like a boat on water and a truck on land. They could carry troops or supplies.

INSTANT DOCKS

Giant harbours were floated across the Channel piece by piece and assembled on site so that ships could unload supplies.

WEIRD TANKS

Several unusual tanks took part in D-Day, including floating tanks, flame-thrower tanks and 'flail' tanks fitted with mine-exploding chains.

A flail tank's roller-mounted chains beat the ground to explode buried mines.

'BLOODY' OMAHA

As they landed, all the invading forces met with fierce resistance from behind coastal defences.

Omaha beach in particular became a killing ground for pinned-down US infantry. German defenders had mined the sea and set up underwater traps that ripped open landing craft, pitching heavily laden troops into the water.

Once they landed, the invaders had to force their way inland to destroy the German defensive gun positions.

By the end of that first day 150,000 Allied troops had landed in Normandy ready to strike into occupied Europe.

US troops wade ashore from a landing craft at Omaha Beach.

The final push

Once the Normandy beaches were secured Allied troops moved inland, fighting the Germans as they went. They met fierce resistance as they pushed towards Germany and had to use heavy bombing and shelling, shattering many towns and villages as they gradually flushed out the occupying Nazi forces.

The Allies were stronger than the Germans, with more equipment. However, Allied commanders disagreed over strategy, giving the Nazis a chance to counter-attack.

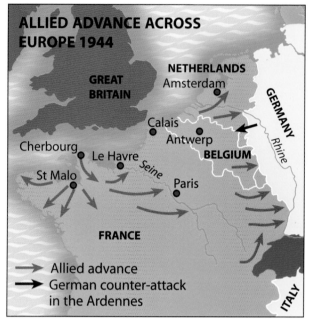

ALLIED ADVANCE ACROSS EUROPE 1944

GREAT BRITAIN

NETHERLANDS
Amsterdam

GERMANY
Rhine

Calais
Antwerp

Cherbourg
Le Havre
Seine

BELGIUM

St Malo

Paris

FRANCE

ITALY

→ Allied advance
→ German counter-attack in the Ardennes

Hand grenade

A German paratrooper fights during the Battle of the Bulge.

THE BATTLE OF THE BULGE

In late 1944 the Germans made a surprise attack to try to retake the city of Antwerp. They drove a wedge through Allied lines in the hilly wooded Ardennes region of Belgium. The 'bulge' they made in the Allied lines gave this battle its name. Eventually they were beaten and the Nazis lost their last gamble.

'We can still lose this war.'

US General Patton warns the Allies during the Battle of the Bulge.

V-1 FLYING BOMB

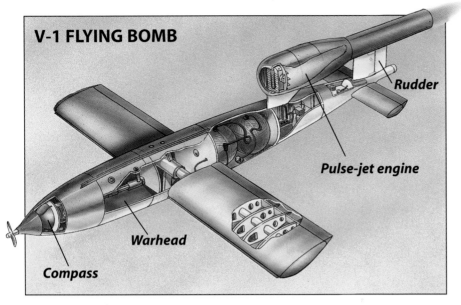

Rudder

Pulse-jet engine

Warhead

Compass

🪖 MADMAN IN CHARGE

By 1944 Adolf Hitler seemed to be losing his mind. He raved madly and took unbalanced decisions, refusing to listen to advice. In 1944 a group of German officers tried to kill him, but their plot was foiled and they were brutally executed.

Meanwhile the Italian fascist leader Mussolini was deposed, hunted down and killed by his own countrymen.

🪖 V-WEAPONS

In 1944 the Nazis began to use a new weapon, the V-1 flying bomb, nicknamed the 'buzz bomb'. These were small pilotless planes packed with explosives and launched from the French coast. They contained just enough fuel to reach London; then their engine cut out and they plummeted to the ground and exploded.

In the winter of 1944 the Nazis also launched a missile called the V-2. Thousands of V weapons dropped on London and other European targets before the war ended.

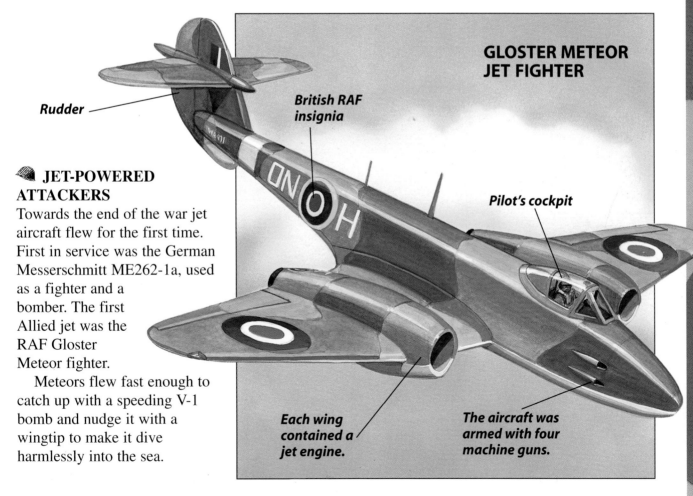

GLOSTER METEOR JET FIGHTER

Rudder

British RAF insignia

Pilot's cockpit

Each wing contained a jet engine.

The aircraft was armed with four machine guns.

🪖 JET-POWERED ATTACKERS

Towards the end of the war jet aircraft flew for the first time. First in service was the German Messerschmitt ME262-1a, used as a fighter and a bomber. The first Allied jet was the RAF Gloster Meteor fighter.

Meteors flew fast enough to catch up with a speeding V-1 bomb and nudge it with a wingtip to make it dive harmlessly into the sea.

End of the war

By the spring of 1945 German forces had collapsed. As Allied troops moved towards Berlin from the west, Stalin's Red Army marched in from the east. Hitler committed suicide on 30 April, leaving his shattered country to the victors, who had to decide what to do with his smashed empire.

The official 'Victory in Europe Day' (VE Day) was 8 May 1945, but the war was not quite over. Japan kept fighting until 14 August; it formally surrendered on 2 September.

Starving Jewish prisoners in a Nazi concentration camp.

THE HUGE COST

Millions of people died in World War Two. Twenty-five million died on the Eastern Front alone. Allied troops went home to rebuild their lives, but some Germans were trapped in USSR labour camps until they died.

MASS MURDER

Advancing Allied troops discovered horrific concentration camps where millions of Jewish people, gypsies and other minorities had been used as slave labour, starved, beaten and executed.

Many were killed in gas chambers; some were used in brutal medical experiments. The camps were run by the SS on Hitler's orders. He believed in 'cleansing' all Nazi territories of minority peoples, whom he hated. He called it the 'Final Solution'. Today it is referred to as the 'Holocaust'.

'The Führer (Hitler) has ordered the final solution of the Jewish question.'

Orders to the commander of Auschwitz concentration camp to kill his prisoners (1941).

VE DAY CELEBRATIONS

In Britain, VE Day was marked by large street party celebrations. But victory did not mean the end of hardship – the war had left thousands of families homeless. Rationing of some items in Britain continued until 1954.

People in Britain held street parties to celebrate the end of the war.

WAR TRIALS

The Allies held war crime trials at Nuremburg. Nazis held responsible for atrocities were tried, convicted and executed.

Some high-ranking Nazis committed suicide rather than face the court. Others escaped and went into hiding.

POSTWAR EUROPE

As the Nazis crumbled, Stalin's communist armies occupied eastern Europe. Europe stayed divided like this until the 1990s. Germany was gradually rebuilt and finally unified as a new democratic nation.

Germany is now a member of the European Union, working closely with its neighbours to ensure peace and prosperity in Europe.

ENOLA GAY

82

Bombs dropped from weapons bay

FIRST NUCLEAR BOMBS

To avoid a prolonged and fiercely fought invasion of Japan, the USA used a newly invented weapon. In August 1945 they dropped nuclear bombs on two Japanese cities, Hiroshima and Nagasaki. The massively powerful bombs killed thousands of people in seconds, shocking the Japanese government into surrender.

The American B-29 bomber Enola Gay dropped the first nuclear bomb.

GLOSSARY

Japanese soldier

Allies
The countries that fought against the Axis powers during World War Two.

ANZAC
Short for the Australia and New Zealand Army Corps – Allied troops from Australia and New Zealand.

Atom bomb
Extremely powerful and devastating type of bomb dropped on Japan to end the war.

Axis powers
Germany, Japan, Italy and some other eastern European countries who fought against the Allies.

Blitz
The nightly bombing of British cities during 1940-41.

Blitzkrieg
The German army's fast advance through Europe in 1939-40. *Blitzkrieg* means 'lightning war'.

Concentration camps
Brutal extermination camps set up by the Nazis to wipe out opponents and people they regarded as 'racially impure'.

Convoy
A group of merchant ships guarded by armed naval vessels.

D-Day
When the Allies landed in France on 6 June 1944 to begin freeing Europe from Nazi occupation.

Eastern Front
The battlefront between Nazi Germany and the USSR.

Führer
The dictator of Germany, Adolf Hitler.

Gestapo
The Nazi secret police.

GIs
A nickname for ordinary American soldiers, short for 'Government Issue', which was stamped on the soldiers' equipment.

Holocaust
The mass murder of millions of Jews and other minorities by the Nazi SS.

Home Front
Wartime life in Britain.

British RAF pilot

Incendiary bomb
A bomb that ignites when it hits the ground, starting a fire.

Kamikaze
Japanese suicide pilots who crashed explosive-packed planes onto enemy ships.

Luftwaffe
The German air force.

Minesweeper
A naval ship fitted with equipment to find and destroy explosive underwater mines.

US infantryman

Nazi
A member of Hitler's National Socialist party and supporter of its policies.

Paravane
A device towed behind a minesweeper. It cut the cable of a floating mine so that the mine could be harmlessly exploded.

Panzer Corps
German army tank units.

POW
Prisoner of war.

RADAR
A detection system that bounces radio waves against a distant object to pinpoint its location.

RAF
The British Royal Air Force.

Red Army
The army of the communist USSR.

Resistance
People in an occupied country who secretly fight their conquerors.

Australian soldier

SS
Nazi military police.

U-boat
German submarine.

USSR
The Union of Soviet Socialist Republics, often referred to as 'Russia'.

V-1/V-2
Pilotless German flying weapons packed with explosives.

Wolfpack
A group of U-boats. They followed ships underwater during the day and surfaced at night to attack.

INDEX

PHOTOGRAPHIC CREDITS

Hulton Getty pp. 9 (Keystone), 10 (Keystone), 15 (Keystone), 22 (Slava Katamidze/Georgi Zelma), 28 (Three Lions)
Peter Newark's Military Pictures pp. 13, 18, 25

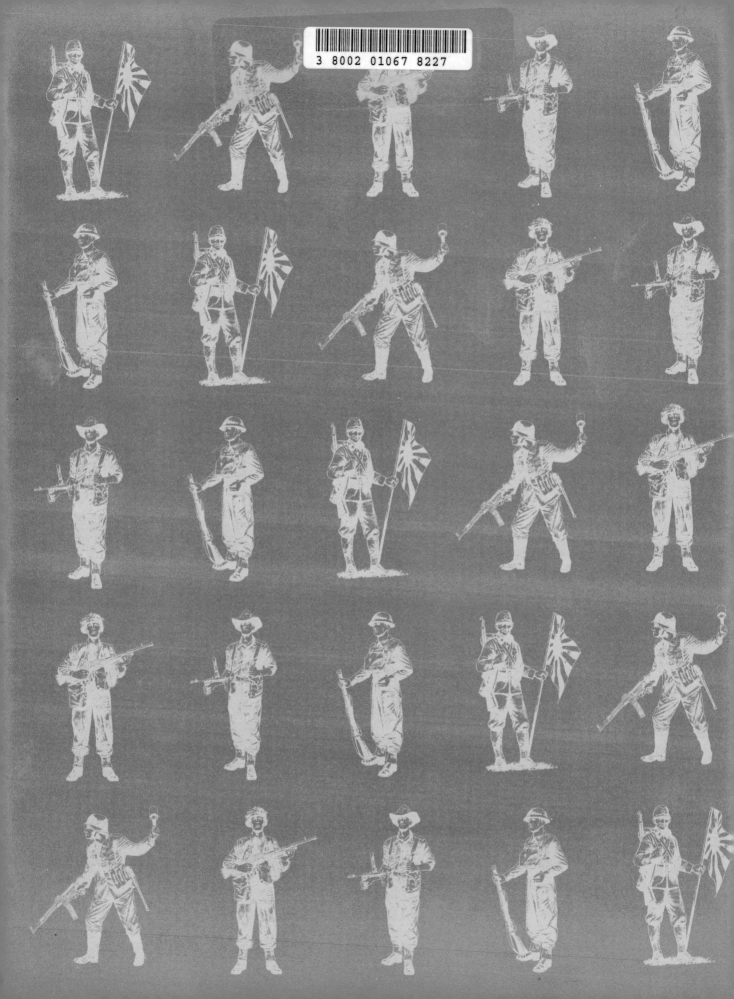